Truth Wins

Conquering Spiritual Warfare Through Christian Apologetics

By Aaron Wentz

Truth Defended Books

Truth Wins

Conquering Spiritual Warfare
Through Christian Apologetics

Aaron Wentz

Apologetic Series Book # 2

©Copyright March 2019
ISBN: 9781090989093
Imprint: Independently published

Please acknowledge all quotes.
Direct permission requests to: Michigansoa@gmail.com

The publisher is not responsible for websites, their content or working condition of the link.
Websites offer resources for further study but are not intended in any way to be,
or imply an endorsement, nor does the publisher vouch for their content.

Scripture taken from: The HOLY BIBLE, NEW INTERNATIONAL VERSION®, NIV®.
Copyright © 1973, 1978, 1984, by Biblica, Inc. ™ Used by permission. All rights reserved worldwide.

Truth Defended Books

Table of Contents

Dedication:

To all my amazing apologetics instructors at Biola University, Thank you for your powerful impact on my life.

Introduction

When Christians hear the words "spiritual warfare" they may think of Jesus encountering demons in his earthly ministry, or stories of missionaries in foreign lands dealing with the bizarre and the supernatural. However, the spiritual warfare currently taking place around the world does not manifest itself primarily in the demonic, *but surprisingly, through the power of ideas.* Ideas, whether good or evil, can create blessings or destruction.

The late philosopher Dallas Willard wrote, "Ideas are very general models of our assumptions about reality. They are ways of thinking about and interpreting things…Examples of ideas may include freedom, education, the American dream, church, democracy, justice, family, God and so on."[1] Willard also wrote concerning the power and influence of ideas that "The killing fields of Cambodia come from the philosophical discussions of Paris."[2] Meaning, ideas are so powerful that the communist ideas formulated by Karl Marx in France later were used to justify totalitarianism and violence in Cambodia.[3]

---

1 www.dwillard.org/articles
2Dallas Willard, *The Divine Conspiracy: Rediscovering our Hidden Life in God* (New York: Harper Collin Publishers, 1998), 7.
3 The teachings of Marxism and totalitarianism deny the worth and freedom of the individual. Josh McDowell and Don Stewart, *Handbook of Today's Religions* (Nashville: Thomas Nelson

Therefore, since ideas are the building blocks of reality, Satan, the author of lies who knows this, uses ideas to accomplish his destructive agenda on earth. To counter Satan's false ideas, apologetics used by the dedicated follower of Christ can defeat Satan's lies, turn a confused person to the truth, and even protect their own faith from satanic deception. Win a lie is replaced by the truth, truth wins, and people are set free.

The purpose of this book is to show how spiritual warfare caused by real spiritual beings, Satan and his demons, can be fought and won by Christians through the use of Christian apologetics.

Publishers, 1983), 449.

Chapter 1: The Fight

The young lady looked at me and said, "Aaron, I don't know what to do."

My mind started to swim as I searched for answers and all I could say was, "Neither do I."

This young lady's name was Kathy, and she was being terrorized by a demon. I was embarrassed because as a Bible college student I had taken classes on angels and demons and didn't know what to do.

Kathy had just gotten saved a few weeks earlier, and now demons were literally standing over her bed night after night harassing her. I told Kathy to tell them to leave in Jesus name, but they kept coming back. I was at a loss. At Kathy's baptism she talked for a half an hour about her horrific ordeal. Thankfully, today she is free. Now is not the time to share everything about Kathy's story, but one big take-away is this: demons are real.

When Christians think of spiritual warfare, they may think of stories like Kathy, or Jesus casting out demons in the Gospel accounts. I'm sure there is the thought, "I hope this never happens to me." And I pray it never does. However, from the opening of the

Bible in Genesis to the close of the Bible in Revelation, the Devil is mentioned.

Since the Devil and demons are real, how do we protect ourselves? Is spiritual warfare just casting out demons, or is it something more? The purpose of this book is to share that yes, demon possession does happen, but it is not the heart of spiritual warfare. When Christians and non-Christians struggle with the Devil and demons it is not just, "There is a demon in my closet! Oh no!" But there is something more.

It is something more hidden and non-obvious, something that we can't see. A battle is being waged in people's minds as to what is true and false. It is a hidden, invisible battle. The battle for truth is a war that leads many to hell or many to eternal life. When the Devil gets a person to believe a lie, he wins. If a person believes God and the Bible, God wins, and the person wins. It is as simple and profound as that. The purpose of this book then, is discussing the essence of what true spiritual warfare is, and how Christian Apologetics, the art of defending the Christian faith, can win the war in people's hearts to believe the Truth.

Before we talk more about how win the war of spiritual warfare, let's introduce who our foe is: the Devil, Satan. Who is he? What is he like? And, where did he come from?

Who is Satan?[4]

A created spirit: Colossians 1:16
An angel: Matthew 25:41, Revelation 12:7
A cherub: Ezekiel 28:14
The highest of all created beings: Ezekiel 28:14

Where did he come from?

- Created perfect: Ezekiel 28:12-13
- Had a heavenly perfect estate: Jude 6
- A guardian of God's glory: Ezekiel 28:14
- The occasion of his sin = power and beauty: Ezekiel 28
- The nature of his sin = pride: Isaiah 14:13, 1 Timothy 3:6
- The cause of sin = personal, free choice: Habakkuk 1:13, James 1:13

Satan's names reveal his tactics:

- Satan (Adversary) Job 1:6-7, 1 Thessalonians 2:18
- Devil (Slanderer) 1 Peter 5:8
- Lucifer (son of the morning) Isaiah 14:12
- Evil One (1 John 5:19)
- Tempter (1 Thessalonians 3:5)

Angels have intellect, emotions and will.

- Angels have intellect: According to1 Peter 1:12, angels long to understand a believer's salvation. Also, angels engage in conversation with humans. (Matthew 1).

---

4   Chip Ingram, *The Invisible War* (Grand Rapids: Baker Publishing, 2006), 19-20.

- Angels have emotions: During creation, angels rejoiced. (Job 38:7) Angels also rejoice at seeing sinners saved. (Luke 15).
- Angels have a will: Each angel had a choice to rebel against God or not.[5]

Demons are fallen angels:

Matthew 25:41 says, "...*the devil and his angels.*"

Demons are evil spirits:

Forty-three times demons are termed *pneuma* or spirits.[6]

Demons have personality:[7]

- Intellect: Demons talk to Jesus and know who He is. (Luke 8:26-39).
- Emotion and will: Demons express fear of being tormented and being sent to a place where they could no longer be active.

What are Satan's Agenda on Earth?

Again, one does not have to look deep into the Bible to find out Satan's agenda on earth. In Genesis chapter 1, God created the universe, and man in his own image (Genesis 1:27). The man God created, Adam is told to take care of the garden to which he was

---

5   Tony Evans, *The Truth about Angels and Demons* (Chicago: Moody Publishing, 2005), 10.
6   C. Fred Dickason, *Angels Elect and Evil* (Chicago: Moody Publishing, 1995), 164.
7   Tony Evans, *The Truth about Angels and Demons*, 10-11.

assigned. There was only one rule; do not eat from the tree of the knowledge of good and evil. If Adam choose to disobey he would die (Genesis 2:16-17). Shortly after the creation of Adam, God wanted a helper for the man, thus creating a woman, Eve.

Now into Genesis 3, Adam and Eve are tested to see if they trusted in God's Word. An animal, specifically a talking serpent of some kind, begins to speak to Eve regarding God's rule about not eating from the Tree of the Knowledge of Good and Evil. To Eve's defense, since she was not there to see all the animals God created in the beginning,[8] she was possibly open to the fact that God might have created an animal with the ability to communicate. In any case, what Adam and Eve did not know was that this serpent, according to Revelation 12:9, was an evil fallen angel whose purpose for being there was to deceive Adam and Eve about God's truth.

The opening chapters of Genesis reveal a lot about the nature of Satan and his tactics in spiritual warfare.

---

8   Genesis 2:1-22 It seems once Adam was finished naming all the
     animals in the Garden of Eden, no suitable helper was found.
     Meaning, of all the amazing creatures God made, none was made
     in the image of God. Therefore, God put Adam to sleep and made
     Eve from one of his ribs. When Eve was then made alive, all the
     animals had been named and put in categories. At the Tree of the
     Knowledge of Good and Evil, Adam should have been Eve's
     protector as he would have known that he had neither seen nor
     named a talking serpent.

First, he uses deception. Satan did not come showing his full glory as a created beautiful angel, but rather he came as a lowly creature, a serpent. In the New Testament, spiritual beings like Satan and demons are able to possess human beings as in the case of Judas (Luke 22:3) and even animals (Mark 5:13).

Second, Satan uses the power of ideas to influence Adam and Eve away from the truth and into a lie. Satan told Eve "you will not surely die..." (Genesis 3:4). Shortly after Adam and Eve disobeyed God, both of them knew they had been deceived.

And third, Satan uses doubt. When Satan said, "Did really say, 'You must not eat from any tree in the garden'?" he was using a lie to make Adam and Eve doubt God's Word and God's goodness (Genesis 3:1).

All three of these tactics are the essence of Satan's war against God and man still today. Jerry Rankin, the former International Missions President of the Southern Baptist Convention who has been a global missionary for thirty years, has written profoundly, "Spiritual warfare is not so much about demon possession, territorial spirits, or generational bondage as it is overcoming Satan's lies and deceits in our own life."[9] Spiritual warfare both then and now manifests through the power of ideas.

---

9 Jerry Rankin, *Spiritual Warfare: The Battle for God's Glory* (Nashville, Tennessee, B&H Publishing, 2009), 8.

From the beginning of Satan's fall until now, Satan has been a liar and uses lies as his main weapon against God and His creation. Jesus said:

"...the devil...he was a murderer from the beginning, not holding to the truth, for there is no truth in him. When he lies, he speaks his native language, for he is a liar and the father of lies." **John 8:44**

Satan's DNA is lies and half-truths. In the Garden of Eden, it was through Satan's lie that sin and death came into the world and the whole universe was brought down. When seeing that Jesus was weak in his human body, Satan lied to Him and twisted Scripture to get Jesus to turn away from God the Father and do His own will. Thankfully, Jesus resisted.

Being a powerful and intelligent angel, Satan knows he doesn't have to do amazing supernatural things to make people turn away from God and hate the truth. As Bible teacher Chip Ingram says, "Satan is always content to hide in the shadows of a world-view if he can exploit that world-view to his own ends."[10] Through false ideas and lies, Satan can actually change a person's view of the world, which in the end becomes a false reality.

---

10 Chip Ingram, *The Invisible War*, 46.

Chapter 2: Why Satanic Lies are so Effective

Because sin has now entered the human race, mankind needs salvation. Christ died for sinners and rose from the dead, which is the gospel message (1 Corinthians 15:1-4). The necessary response to Jesus' offer of a free pardon is to believe the great news that forgiveness is possible, and that reconciliation with God is available through His Son, Jesus Christ. Acts 16:31 says, *"Believe on the Lord Jesus Christ and you will be saved."* Once salvation occurs, a non-believer who has now become a believer in Christ as his Savior actually transfers out of Satan's power into God's family and protection. Colossians 1:13-14 says:

"For he has rescued us from the dominion of darkness and brought us into the kingdom of the Son he loves, in whom we have redemption, the forgiveness of sins."

Since salvation through faith in Jesus Christ is so important, theologians have explained saving faith in three levels:

1. Knowledge:

For salvation to occur, a person first has to hear the gospel and understand the basic ideas and truths about God, sin, Jesus, the after-life, etc. In Romans 10, the Apostle Paul makes the case that mission work is necessary because someone can't call on the One about whom they have not heard. Knowledge, therefore, is the first step in saving faith.

2. Belief:

Once a person hears and understands God's plan of salvation, he has the choice to believe whether the ideas he heard are true or false. Again, in Romans 10, the Apostle Paul reminds the church in Rome that the Jews heard the gospel through Christ but chose not to believe.

3. Trust or Commitment:

When a sinner hears the good news, understands it and believes the message is true, the next step God asks people to do is to personally trust in Jesus as their Savior as an act of their will. Theologians often use the chair analogy. It is one thing to believe that a chair exists, or even that the chair will hold you, but to physically sit down and trust your life to that chair takes faith as an act of the will. Again, the Apostle Paul explains trust as when the person finally "...calls on the name of the Lord..." he will be saved, Romans 10:13.

Therefore, saving faith could be explained by this formula:

Biblical knowledge and ideas leads to reason, reason leads to understanding, understanding leads to belief, belief leads to trust, and trusting Christ leads to salvation.

Because the gospel and saving faith are the means by which God snatches people out of Satan's kingdom, it makes sense that the point of satanic attack strikes at knowledge and reason, which are the very foundation of faith. Philosopher Peter Kreeft [11] explains why so well:

"Reason is a friend, not an enemy, to faith for it is a road to truth and a means to loving God, who is Truth. Arguments, ideas and reasoning get at the heart through the head. The head is important precisely because it is a gate to the heart. We can love only what we know. Further, reason at least has veto power. We can't believe what we know to be untrue, and we can't love what we believe to be unreal. Arguments may not bring you to faith, but they can certainly keep you away from faith."[12]

As Kreeft says, "…reason has veto power" and Satan knows this. All it takes is for Satan to produce a lie about God, such as the Bible being corrupted, Jesus not rising from the dead, right and wrong being subjective, etc., and as a result, Satan has replaced true

---

[11] Even though Dr. Kreeft is quoted in this paper as philosopher for apologetics, I do not endorse his teachings as a Roman Catholic, such as salvation and Biblical authority.

[12] Peter J. Kreeft, *Handbook of Catholic Apologetics* (San Francisco: Ignatius Press, 2009), 23-24

knowledge with false knowledge. If a person thinks that God does not exist, the Bible is corrupted, Jesus never existed, and morals don't matter, and Christianity is fairy tales, they will never come to trust their life to Jesus.

Jesus said Satan is not only the Father of lies, but also a murderer (John 8:44). If Satan can get a person to believe a lie, and therefore ultimately reject the love of God in the gospel, then Satan has successfully murdered them, since he has killed the only way for a person to escape death and have eternal life.

Three ways Satan transfers his lies to humans

Satan is a person. One does not have to have a physical or human body to be a person. God is a person and has all the qualities of personhood without having a physical body. Likewise, Satan has all the qualities of a person even though he has no permanent physical body. He is a spiritual being. Knowing this is important because Satan is not a thing or a force, but an invisible person whose very nature is evil and wants to destroy people's lives. Jesus said, *"The thief comes only to steal, kill and destroy; I have come that they may have life..."* (John 10:10). Satan spreads his lies to steal, kill, and destroy someone's faith in three ways:

1. Frontal Attack:

In the Old Testament, Satan came directly at Adam and Eve with his false idea about God. In the Gospels, Satan once again appeared in a frontal attack, but this time he had the gall to take on the Son of God (Matthew 4). In the New Testament letter to the church in Galatia, the Apostle Paul warned the new believers that it could be possible for an angel to appear and give a message contrary to the gospel message Paul preached. Paul warned the church not to believe it, if an angel did appear with a different gospel, especially a gospel of works (Galatians 1:6-9). 1 Peter 5:8 says Satan is like a lion actively looking for someone to devour. And in the Old Testament book of Job, Satan appeared before God in heaven to accuse a righteous man on earth named Job. When God asked Satan where he had been, Satan replied that he had been roaming the earth. It is clear from these passages that Satan is active on the earth.

2. Direct Contact to the Mind:

Just as God can speak to the heart and mind of man, it seems clear from the Scriptures that Satan, being a spiritual being, can speak to the spirit or minds of men to plant lies, doubts, and fears. In the Old Testament, in 1 Chronicles 21:1, Satan somehow planted the idea in David's mind to take a census of all Israel, which was a sin in the sight of God. In Mark 8:31-33, Jesus rebuked Satan, but looked at Peter while doing the rebuking. Why? Peter's thought of Jesus not going to the cross did not originate with himself, but with Satan.

Also, In Acts 5, the Apostle Peter had to rebuke and discipline two people, Ananias and Sapphira in their church for lying. Peter said, "Ananias, how is it that Satan has so filled your heart that you have lied to the Holy Spirit..." (Acts 5:1-4). So, Ananias carried out the lie to the church, but the original lie came from Satan himself.

3. Worldly Influences:

All over the world, information comes across the minds of people through books, magazines, college classrooms, internet, movies, friends, etc. For Satan to perpetuate a lie today all he needs is the vehicle or people to spread his false ideas like a contagious disease. The DaVinci Code is an example of Satan using the power and popularity of books and movies to spread lies about Jesus, and the Bible being corrupted. Brown used false assumptions to build his theme, and presented them as foundational truth upon which he developed the rest of the book. Unlike any other time in history, Satan's lies can be spread quickly through all forms of media.

> Ephesians 2:1-2 says, *"...you followed the **ways of this world** and of the ruler of the kingdom of the air, the spirit who is now at work in those who are disobedient."* And 1 John 5:19 says, *"...the **whole world** is under the control of the evil one."*

What does the Bible teach as the answer to combat the power of the enemy? In the same passage where Satan is on the move to destroy the lives of people (1 Peter 5:8), the answer is found in verse 9 where it says, *"Resist him, standing firm in the faith..."* The ability of a Christian to counter the attack of the enemy is by standing firm in the truth of the Christian faith. A Christian who is convinced about *what* he believes and *why* he believes it, this is a person not easily moved by lies.

However, what about non-Christians? They are an easy target of the enemy, since most people do not know what the truth from the Holy Scriptures is, or why it is true, especially if they have been raised from birth on ideas that are contrary to Christian doctrine.

How then can a Christian help people who know the truth and have been taken captive by Satan's lies, whether by direct false teaching from Satan himself, lies to their minds, or worldly influences? The answer is what Christians call "The Great Commission." Before Jesus ascended to heaven, He reminded and commissioned the early disciples about their mission on earth:

"All authority in heaven and on earth has been given to me. Therefore, go and make disciples of all nations, baptizing them in the name of the Father and of the Son and of the Holy Spirit, and teaching them to obey everything I have commanded you. And surely, I am with you always, to the very end of the age." Matthew 28:18-20.

A few years after Jesus ascended into heaven and the gospel was preached, a persecutor of the church was saved and he changed his name from Saul to Paul. When Jesus commissioned the Apostle Paul to reach the Gentile world with the good news, Jesus Himself told Paul these words:

> *"I am sending you to them to open their eyes and turn them from darkness to light and from the power of Satan to God, so that they may receive forgiveness of sins and a place among those who are sanctified by faith in me."* Acts 26:18

It is clear then, from Jesus' own words to the Apostle Paul, the heart of sharing the gospel is a spiritual battle, or spiritual warfare. What is assumed from Acts 26:18 is that everyone outside of the saving power of Jesus Christ is under the influence and power of Satan. And how does Satan keep people captive in his kingdom and influence? The answer again is simple: lies. Satan's lies bring people into bondage as well as keep them there through false ideas and beliefs.

Chapter 3: Apologetics Helps in Spiritual Warfare

Jesus gave the Great Commission to all Christians to rescue people from the power of Satan. The difficulty faced by Christians all over the world as they try to witness and call people to repent and believe the gospel, is that billions of people don't have the foundational concepts or beliefs to even consider the claims of Christianity to be true. Again, as philosopher Peter Kreeft said, "…we can't love what we believe to be unreal."[13] Here are two real-life examples of the power of Satan's lies that attack the foundational knowledge, reason, and understanding of Christianity:

The number one lie that has destroyed the need for Christ in the West: Evolution.

Charles Darwin and his ideas of biological evolution via natural selection spun the lie that the Genesis account of creation is false and God is not the Creator. Professor Phillip E. Johnson rightly wrote, "The discovery of evolution finally made possible the 'death' of God, with Charles Darwin supplying the indispensable murder weapon. This was the theory of natural selection, which made God unnecessary as Creator in the living world…belief in a personal,

---

13   Peter Kreft, *Handbook of Catholic Apologetics*, 24.

supernatural Creator is increasingly confined to the uneducated..."[14] Basically what Charles Darwin's theory did was an attempt to kill God. The rational conclusion behind his theory can lead one to think, if there is no God, and then Jesus is not God, and did not rise from the dead. Therefore, there is no after-life such as heaven or hell. If evolution is true and there is no God, Christianity is totally irrelevant.

The number one lie that has destroyed the need for Christ in the East: Islam.

Some of the basic teaching of Islam is that Jesus is not God and that Jesus did not die on the cross and rise from the dead. In fact, Jesus is just a prophet. Even more degrading than that low status, Jesus is not even the last and the best prophet. According to Islam, the Bible predicted the coming of the prophet Muhammad as the final messenger, bringing the final revelation of God to earth. Jesus is respected in Islam, but the need to study the words of Jesus is irrelevant since the final and complete truth was given in the Quran through the prophet Muhammad. Sadly, over a billion people on earth believe these ideas to be true.

Therefore, as stated earlier, if saving faith is in three crucial stages (knowledge, belief, and trust) then Satan's lies have destroyed

14   Philip E. Johnson, *The Right Questions: Truth, Meaning and Public Debate* (Downers Grove, IL: Intervarsity Press, 2002), 65.

the credibility of Christianity at its foundation. In the West, if not in most of Europe, the call to belief in Jesus as Savior is now nonsense since evolution/naturalism has made the need for God obsolete. In the East, the command to repent and believe the good news is considered foolish to the Muslim who has God's "final" revelation. This is true spiritual warfare. And as Jerry Rankin says, it is all over a battle for God's glory.[15] *"Who will be glorified God, or Satan? And the battle is waged in the arena of ideas."*

How does a Christian help a non-Christian of any sort begin to see the value of the Word of God, Jesus Christ and his death and resurrection? First, never neglect preaching and teaching the gospel. The Holy Spirit is the invisible power source that can convict and open the mind of any unbeliever. And second, pre-evangelism must be done in many situations to bring true understanding and true knowledge to a mind that has been plagued with lies by Satan.

Basically, the battle plan is simple: replace the lies of Satan with God's truth.

If a person has heard the lie that there is no God, it's necessary to replace the lie with true knowledge about the reality of God's existence. If a person has been lied to, thinking that the Bible isn't worth reading because it has been corrupted over thousands of

---

15   Jerry Rankin, *Spiritual Warfare: The Battle for God's Glory*, 8.

years, replace the lie with true knowledge about the inspiration and veracity of the Scriptures. If a person has been lied to that Jesus is not God, and the resurrection of Jesus is a myth made up by Christian legend, we must replace the lies with the truth that the resurrection of Jesus Christ is one of the best attested to events in ancient history. *This method is what Christians call apologetics.*

What is Apologetics?

In Philippians 1:16 the Apostle Paul says he was placed in jail "...*knowing that I am put here for the **defense** of the gospel.*" The English word "defense" is derived from the Greek word *apologia,* which in the first century referred to a legal defense. Greek scholar Kenneth Wuest wrote that the word *apologia* "was a technical word in the Greek law courts used to designate the work of a lawyer, one who presented a verbal defense for his client, proving that the charge preferred against his client was not true." Wuest concludes by writing, "The Bible today is being charged with being a man-made book, full of inaccuracies, a mass of myths and fairy tales.

Christians are exhorted to present a verbal defense for the Bible, proving that the charge is not true."[16]

---

16   Kenneth Wuest, *Wuest's Word Studies From the Greek New Testament* (Grand Rapids: Eerdmans Publishing, 1973), 94.

1 Peter 3:15 says "...*always be prepared to give an answer (apologia) to everyone who asks you to give the reason for the hope that you have...*" Jude reminded and challenged his readers to "*contend for the faith that was once for all entrusted to the saints*" (Jude 3).[17]

A real life example of how apologetics is being used today is through people like Dr. William Lane Craig, one of the world's foremost apologists. All over the world Dr. Craig contends for the faith and tears down lies that challenge God and His Word through his writing, speaking, and public debates at well-known universities. Here is the way Dr. Craig explains the purpose of apologetics:

"Apologetics is that branch of Cristian theology that seeks to provide rational warrant for Christianity's truth claims. It contains offensive and defensive elements, on the one hand presenting positive arguments for Christian truth claims and on the other refuting objections brought against Christianity's truth claims."[18]

If a thoughtful and well-informed Christian does not stand up against the barrage of objections brought against Christianity, then who will? Satan would love nothing more than to keep putting lies out into the culture with no one to stand up and say why they are

---

17   Sean McDowell et al., *Apologetics for a New Generation* (Eugene, Oregon: Harvest House Publishers, 2009), 17.
18   William Lane Craig et al., *To Everyone An Answer* (Downers Grove, IL: Intervarsity Press, 2004), 19.

wrong. If no one will defend Christ and defeat the objections that come from the mind of the enemy, then the enemy wins, and souls are lost because they believe lies instead of the truth that will save their souls.

Another soldier for Christ in the area of apologetics has been Dr. Norman Geisler. Dr. Geisler has been defending the faith publicly for over fifty years. Perhaps his definition of apologetics makes it clear enough for everyone to understand why apologetics is so needed. Dr. Geisler said apologetics "…is opening the door, clearing the rubble, and getting rid of the hurdles so that people can come to Christ."[19]

What is beautiful about Dr. Geisler's definition of apologetics is how he sees it clearly used in the purpose of evangelism to the glory of God. The "closed door, rubble, and hurdles" of which he speaks all represent the roadblocks Satan has created, so people won't walk through the "gospel door" and find Christ, who can free them from Satan's lies and bring them into God's kingdom. When a person turns from Satan's lies and embraces Jesus' truth, God is glorified and Satan is defeated. Without apologetics opening the door, clearing the rubble and getting rid of the hurdles, Satan's deception wins, and Satan is glorified in the ruining of another human life. Therefore, since

---

19   Quoted in: *To Everyone An Answer*, 9.

apologetics is the noble task of replacing Satan's lies with God's truth, it is absolutely crucial in evangelism and missions in the world today.

Chapter 4: An Apologetic for Apologetics

Since apologetics is very crucial in spiritual warfare, it would make sense that Satan would promote lies about apologetics! As with the Apostle Peter, even well-meaning Christians are not immune from a satanic thought. When Peter thought his idea of keeping Jesus from the cross was noble, Jesus rebuked his idea as satanic. Christians today, if not aware of the nature of spiritual warfare, can become easily duped into believing a satanic lie pertaining to apologetics. Satan would probably love nothing more than the church to become impotent by believing that evangelism and apologetics are not necessary. Therefore, an apologetic for apologetics is needed. Here are six false ideas about apologetics:

1. Apologetics is unbiblical

The fact is, two New Testament books were written to combat false ideas that had the potential of destroying the early church. The Apostle Paul wrote the letter to the Galatians to protect them against the false ideas of the Judaizers, who taught that keeping the Ten Commandments and circumcision were necessary for salvation. Also, the Apostle John wrote the book of 1 John as an apologetic against the teachings of Gnosticism which tried to cripple the Divinity and humanity of Jesus.[20] Even Jesus gave many

---

20   Ken Samples, *Without a Doubt* (Grand Rapids, MI: Baker Books, 2004), 255-256.

convincing proofs that he was alive after his crucifixion and resurrection from the dead (Acts 1:1-3).

2. Christians just need to preach the gospel

First, the Apostle Paul at times needed to defend the gospel as seen in Philippians 1 and his sermon in the pagan city of Athens, Greece (Acts 17). Therefore, to say Christians need to only preach the gospel is unbiblical. Second, saving faith starts with knowledge, sound reasoning, and understanding. Since Satan is very active in using false knowledge and false reasoning to create a wrong understanding of God and the Bible and Truth and Jesus, apologetics is necessary to repair and restore what Satan has destroyed, through teaching God's truth to make a reasonable foundation as to why Christianity should be believed.

3. Apologetics, using arguments, and giving reasons doesn't save anyone

One would have to have all knowledge to know that apologetics has never saved or been used to win someone to Christ. In fact, the opposite is true. One of the most influential Christian thinkers and writers, C.S. Lewis, was profoundly impacted by apologetics and sound reasoning prior to his conversion.

Also, if Satan gives false reasons not to believe in Jesus, why shouldn't Christians give positive reasons to believe in Jesus? Finally, Peter Kreeft wisely wrote:

"Arguments may not bring you to faith, but they can certainly keep you away from faith. Therefore, we must join the battle of arguments. Arguments can bring you to faith in the same sense as a car can bring you to the sea. The car can't swim; you have to jump in to do that. But you can't jump in from a hundred miles inland. You need a car first to bring you to the point where you can make a leap of faith into the sea."[21]

4. People come to Christ through experience, not reason.

Peter Kreeft writes again on this subject by stating, "Most of us know that our heart is our center, not our head. But apologetics gets at the heart *through* the head. The head is important precisely because it is the gate to the heart. We can only love what we know."[22]

5. Apologetics is too intellectual and abstract.

Again, Peter Kreeft writes: "Most people scorn or ignore apologetics because it seems very intellectual, abstract and rational. They contend that life and love and morality and sanctity are much more important than reason. Those who reason this way are right;

---

21   Peter Kreeft, *Handbook of Catholic Apologetics*, 24.
22   Ibid., 24.

they just don't notice that they are reasoning. We can't avoid doing it – we can only avoid doing it well. Further, reason is a friend, not an enemy to faith."[23]

6. Christians shouldn't argue with people.

If the word "argue" means yelling at people, then Scripture seriously frowns on this behavior since Christians are to defend the faith with gentleness and respect (1 Peter 3:15). But the word "argue" in the philosophical use of the word means to bring forth a set of arguments or premises that lead to a conclusion. An example would be in a court of law when a lawyer defends his position with evidence to make the conclusion that his client is not guilty. An argument is only valid when its conclusion follows from its premises.[24]

Therefore, since Satan tells lies, Christians, out of compassion, need to rescue people from Satan's lies by replacing the lie with the truth. The only way Christians can be on the offensive and help people in this "truth war" is to "argue" or bring forth true statements that lead to the conclusion that God's Word's and His Son are true.

---

23   Ibid., 24.
24   Ted Honderrich ed., *The Oxford Companion to Philosophy* (New York: Oxford University Press, 2005), 49.

Dr. Clay Jones, Associate Professor of Christian Apologetics at Biola University, has brilliantly written on this exact subject and why Christians need to argue or fight against Satan and his lies. Dr. Jones' words below, taken from his internet blog: "*Arguing doesn't do any good? Sure it does!*" are worth reading, as it is the highlight argument of this paper. Dr. Jones writes:

"We've all heard someone say, People shouldn't argue. Well, my answer to that is to ask, Can you give me some reasons for why you believe that? Of course the reason is: because arguing doesn't do any good. To this I will point out that they have just argued. After all, argue simply means to give reasons for what you believe, and that is exactly what they have done.

Look, People shouldn't argue is just another one of Satan's talking points that his minions (and sometimes even some Christians!) mindlessly blabber. Now, if argue meant two people screaming and neither listening, then I'm against it. But since argue means to give reasons for what you believe, then that is precisely what we should be doing. If anything, many Christians should do it much more than they do. Consider that Christ and the apostles argued a lot and, well, WWJD, then we should too.

After all, what exactly do we think was going on when Jesus talked to the Pharisees? Arguing, right? And usually the Pharisees got really mad. They accused Jesus of being a demon possessed blasphemer and sometimes they tried to stone him or push him off of a cliff.

And the apostles were no different. Two examples should suffice. In Acts 19:8 we read that Paul entered the synagogue and spoke boldly there for three months, arguing [*dialegomai*] persuasively about the kingdom of God. Then in Acts 17:2-3 it says, As his custom was, Paul went into the synagogue, and on three Sabbath days he reasoned [*dialegomai*] with them from the Scriptures, explaining and proving that the Christ had to suffer and rise from the dead. As is the case with the NIV, translations might render *dialegomai* sometimes as *argue* and other times as *reason* but it's the same Greek word. Of course, what's at stake here is significant. Would the devil like anything more than when someone challenged the truth of historic Christianity, we just sat silent while quoting to ourselves the maxim people shouldn't argue?

On the contrary, what the church needs is many people trained to defend the truths of historic Christianity. Answering tough questions is a great encouragement to the church. For example, consider Acts 18:27-28: When Apollos wanted to go to Achaia; the brothers encouraged him and wrote to the disciples there to welcome him. On arriving, he was a great help to those who by grace had believed, for he vigorously refuted the Jews in public debate, proving from the Scriptures that Jesus was the Christ. Don't we need more Christians like Apollos? 1 Pet. 3:15: Always be prepared to give an answer to everyone who asks you to give the reason for the hope that you have. But do this with gentleness and respect."[25]

---

25   http://www.clayjones.net/2010/09/arguing-doesn%e2%80%99t-do-any-good-sure-it-does/

Chapter 5: A Biblical Exposition on Spiritual Warfare

The Apostle Paul wrote in 2 Corinthians 10:3-5:

"For though we walk in the flesh, we do not war according to the flesh, for the weapons of our warfare are not of the flesh, but divinely powerful for the destruction of fortresses. We are destroying speculations and every lofty thing raised up against the knowledge of God, and we are taking every thought captive to the obedience of Christ."

The following biblical interpretations on 2 Corinthians 10:3-5 are from International Bible teacher and author John MacArthur, based on his commentary on 2 Corinthians.[26] The biblical text of 2 Corinthians 10:3-5, according to MacArthur, is the foundation for understanding spiritual warfare and teaches that people are in a war (*strateuomai).* In the Greek this word means "to engage in battle."

The battle is not a physical battle but a spiritual battle. MacArthur wrote, "All believers are soldiers in the spiritual warfare against the kingdom of darkness. They fight for the truth of

---

26   John MacArthur, *The MacArthur New Testament Commentary* (Chicago: Moody Press, 2003), 130-136.

Scripture, the honor and glory of the Lord Jesus Christ, the salvation of sinners, and the virtue of the saints." The word "fortress" could mean a high wall like the wall of the acropolis. But, according to MacArthur, in extra-Biblical Greek literature the word "fortress" (*ochuroma*) could also mean prison or tomb. Not only is the spiritual battle to destroy these fortresses, but speculations and "every lofty thing" that challenges God. The word speculation (*logismos*) means "any and all human or demonic thoughts, opinions, reasoning, philosophies, theories, psychologies, perspectives, view points and religions."

Putting all this together then, MacArthur says, "The battle is rather with the false ideologies men and demons propagate so that the world believes them." The Apostle Paul's analogy of the spiritual battle being a battle of tearing down "fortresses" and destroying speculations means:

> "Doomed souls are inside their fortresses of ideas, which become their prisons and eventually their tombs – unless they are delivered from them by belief in the truth...There is the key. Spiritual warfare is not a battle with demons. It is a battle for the minds of people who are captive to the lies that are exalted in opposition to Scripture...Like Paul, before salvation, all unbelievers have a fortress in which they attempt to hide from the true knowledge of God."

The goal then is to take wrong ideas, false teachings and make them captive to the obedience of Christ. The words "take captive" (*aichmalotizo)* in the Greek literally mean to "take captive with a spear." The only spiritual weapon that is capable of capturing and killing a lie is God's truth. Only the truth can turn a person from false ideas to salvation. The word *obedient,* according to MacArthur, is a synonym for *salvation.*

The Apostle Paul gives similar analogy of spiritual warfare in Ephesians 6:10-20 of a Christian being suited like a soldier ready for battle. Each piece of armor is given a spiritual analogy to fight the spiritual war. The Apostle Paul taught that the soldier's shield is analogous to faith. Just as a shield stops a flaming arrow from hitting the soldier, a Christian's faith in God stops Satan's lies from hurting or killing the Christian. Of all the pieces of a Roman soldier's armor, the belt was the centerpiece of the armor. The Roman soldier's belt would hold together all the pieces and stabilize the armor. Also, on the belt the soldiers would hang their sword and daggers. Since the Apostle understood the uses of a soldier's armor, he applied the belt to truth calling it "the belt of truth" (Ephesians 6:14). To win the spiritual war, truth is central and foundational. The devil uses lies to defeat men, and Christians protect themselves from Satan's lies by knowing the truth. Again, if the sword hangs on "the belt of truth" and the sword represents "the Word of God," then Christians, as their offensive weapon against the devil, are hacking down the lies of the enemy using the Word of God as their source of truth.[27] In many ways, then, apologetics represents the belt of truth in the spiritual battle as God commands believers to defend the truth, use it against Satan's lies.

---

27   Tony Evans, *Victory in Spiritual Warfare* (Eugene, Oregon: Harvest House Publishers, 2011), 55.

Chapter 6: Apologetics Helps Unbelievers See the Truth

It has been shown that Satan attacks people in three primary ways:

1) Frontal attack.

2) Direct contact to the mind.

3) Worldly influences.

Here are some practical ways apologetics helps in spiritual warfare:

1. Frontal Attack.

Satan made a frontal assault on Adam and Eve and on Jesus Himself, as mentioned earlier. The Apostle Paul warned the church "…even if we or an angel from heaven should preach a gospel other than the one we preached to you, let him be eternally condemned". (Galatians 1:8). Sometime in the late sixth century, an angel named Gabriel came to a man in Arabia named Muhammad. The angel told Muhammad that he was God's final prophet on earth to bring God's final revelation on earth.[28] Over a period of twenty years this same angel gave Muhammad 114 Surah's, or revelations, which later became the Qur'an.[29] Part of this revelation from the angel Gabriel

---

28   Suzanne Haneef, *What Everyone Should Know About Islam and Muslims* (Library of Islam, 1996), 20.

29   Caesar E. Farah, *Islam* (Hauppauge, New York: Barron's Educational Series, 1994), 95.

was that Jesus was not God, and Jesus never died on the cross. The Qur'an states in Surah 4:157, "They slew him not nor crucified him, but it appeared so unto them…" Most Muslims believe Judas died in the place of Jesus, and Christ went to heaven and escaped death.[30]

How is a Christian going to answer the claims of a believer in Islam that their faith was started by a false God (Allah)? First, if a Christian knows the truth, he or she can defend the truth, which again is what apologetics is all about. A well-informed Christian, just from reading the New Testament should catch that an angel did appear and gave another gospel. The angel that called himself "Gabriel" of course was Satan in a deceptive frontal attack. 2 Corinthians 11:14 says "And no wonder, for Satan himself masquerades as an angel of light." Again, Satan's attack was not done through force or even fear, but rather by telling Muhammad lies about God, Jesus, and salvation for over twenty years; and this has more than one billion people deceived.

How should a Christian defend the faith that Jesus did indeed die on the cross? It is this kind of problem that makes apologetics so necessary. Apologist Dr. Michael Licona answers this problem, calling it "The Islamic Catch 22." The argument goes like this:

"If Jesus did not die a violent and imminent death, then that makes him a false prophet. But the Qur'an says that he's a great

---

30   Josh McDowell, *Handbook of Today's Religions*, 395.

prophet, and so the Qur'an would be wrong and thus discredited. On the other hand, if Jesus did die a violent and imminent death as he predicted, then he is indeed a great prophet – but this would contradict the Qur'an, which says he didn't die on the cross. So either way, the Qur'an is discredited."[31]

2. Direct Contact to the Mind.

As mentioned earlier, In Acts 5:1-3, Satan planted a lie into the minds of Ananias and Sapphira. Today the amount of deception, lies, and false teaching is too abundant to categorize. At any moment, a demon can plant a lie into the mind of a person, hoping they will believe the lie instead of the truth. Especially if a person doesn't know very much biblical truth, believing a satanic lie would be easy. One easy lie for the devil to get away with would be, "Jesus never rose from the dead. The disciples stole the body and made up the story of the resurrection." Apologist Ken Samples answers this objection well with a logical and historical argument:

"And what possible motivation would the apostles have had for stealing the body? They had nothing to gain and everything to lose by doing so. Creating a hoax about Jesus' resurrection could only bring them meaningless hardship, persecution, martyrdom, and even possible damnation for blasphemy. If the Apostles had, in fact,

---

31   Quoted in Lee Strobel, *Finding the Real Jesus* (Grand Rapids: Zondervan, 2008), 71.

stolen the body and then created a hoax concerning the resurrection appearances, would they then be willing to die as martyrs for what they knew was false? Such a conspiracy would likely have come apart under pressure."[32]

3. Worldly Influences.

Like a rat carrying bacteria that caused black plague in the Middle Ages, Satan sends out his lies carried by television, movies, music, books, college classrooms, etc., all over the world. In the western hemisphere ideas such as relativism, pluralism, and naturalism have suffocated the life out of Christianity. These simple ideas below have, as philosopher Paul Copan says, left Christians speechless.

"All truth is relative."

"There is no absolute truth."

"It's true for you, not true for me."

"You can't know anything for sure."

"Truth can't be known."

"All religious beliefs are true."

"Christians are intolerant."

---

32   Ken Samples, *Without a Doubt*, 142-143.

"You shouldn't judge."

The above ideas are powerful because they twist the truth and confuse people. Just like in the Garden of Eden, Satan twisted the truth just enough to make Eve confused. Thankfully, many godly and smart theologians, philosophers, and apologists have tackled these pluralistic and relativistic ideas and shown them to be false. Here is how apologist Dr. Frank Turek answers these statements in his book, *I Don't Have Enough Faith to be an Atheist*.[33]

"All truth is relative." Really, is *that* a relative truth?

"There is no absolute truth." Are you *absolutely* sure?

"It's true for you, but not true for me." Is that statement true just for me, or is it true for everyone?

"You can't know anything for sure." How do you know *that* for sure?

"Truth can't be known." How do you *know* that?

"All religious beliefs are true." What about the religious beliefs that believes that that statement is false?

---

33   Frank Turek, *I Don't Have Enough Faith To Be An Atheist* (Wheaton, Illinois: Crossway Books, 2004), 40-47.

"Christians are intolerant." Aren't you imposing your view on me right now? That's not very tolerant of you, is it?

"You shouldn't judge." Why are you are judging me right now, then?

Apologetics has the ability to replace a satanic lie with truth. Once a person thinks clearly, reasons clearly, and understands the foundations of Christianity, then true belief can arise which can lead to personal trust in Jesus Christ.

Chapter 7: Apologetics and Spiritual Warfare

So far this book has dealt with Christians using apologetics to help non-Christians. But how can apologetics help a Christian who struggles with spiritual warfare?

1. Frontal Attack:

When banks and the government train people to spot counterfeit money, they have them study only real money so that when they see a counterfeit they will know it instantly.

Millions of Mormons call themselves Christians, but in a similar way to Islam, the foundation of their religion started with an angel appearing to a man in the 1800's named Joseph Smith in Vermont, claiming he was God's final prophet to bring God's true revelation to the earth. Many Christians today are being led astray by Mormons and their cultic doctrines. When Christians know what they believe and why they believe it, this knowledge can keep an individual or a family from turning to a cult. 2 Corinthians 11 makes it clear that Satan uses slick and masterful men and women as false teachers to lead people away from the gospel and into satanic lies. Knowing the truth through studying apologetics, theology, cults, and false religions can save individuals, families, and churches from Satan's destructive lies.

2. Direct Contact to the Mind.

As stated earlier, if a dedicated follower like Peter could be influenced mentally by Satan, why wouldn't a Christian today also be able to be similarly influenced by Satan? Peter, in his own epistle, says to watch out and stand firm in the faith since the devil prowls around like a lion looking for someone to devour (1 Peter 5:8-9).

Emotional doubt is a strong defeater for many Christians. Godly people are not immune to sickness, cancer, persecution, or even the premature death of children. Peter uses the imagery of Satan as a lion; lions attack weak, hurting, and young animals. Christians are especially vulnerable to satanic attack during times of emotional and physical turmoil. Again, Satan's attacks come in the form of lies, doubts, and accusations. During times of emotional stress, it is common for Satan to say to the mind of a Christian, "How do you know God loves you?" "If God loved you, you wouldn't be going through this right now." "The reason why God isn't answering your prayers is because He doesn't exist." "Just walk away from the church, Christianity has never been true anyway." Apologetics can help in these kinds of situations by showing how those statements are lies.

One godly couple explained how apologetics helped them in their darkest moments.[34] Somewhat early on in their marriage they lost two babies at separate times. The husband commented that at night he would lie awake and doubt so much, that he wanted to leave the faith. "How could God let this happen?" he would wonder. However, he had studied apologetics early on in his Christian life and said, "The only thing that kept me from walking away from God in those dark times of pain and doubt was the inner presence of the Holy Spirit in my heart and the evidence for the resurrection. Though my heart told me to leave the faith, my mind told me that because of the historical proofs of the resurrection, leaving the faith would be suicide. There was no other explanation for the empty tomb in history that made sense to me." This was a great example of how God uses apologetics, giving evidence to ground the emotions in reality when the world turns upside down.

3. Worldly Influences.

The book of 2 Timothy predicts that in the end days, there won't be a world-wide revival but instead spiritual darkness. Part of this darkness, Timothy says in chapter 3, is that people won't be lovers of God and will abandon sound doctrine. As Christian families raise their children today, it is not enough to take them to church and have them hear Bible stories like David and Goliath.

Children by the fourth grade will be impacted by evolution, pluralism, relativism, materialism, and secularism. Especially in middle school and into high school, if Christian families do not teach apologetics to their children, their faith will be shaken, if not defeated by the power of the world's influences through Satan's ideas mainstreamed into all parts of society. Thankfully, today there is a bountiful supply of books and videos to equip children, teenagers, and families to know what they believe and why they believe it.

Conclusion

Until Jesus returns, Satan and his demons will be alive and active on planet earth. His tactics have been, and always will be to use deception, doubt, and lies to get people to turn away from God. The only remedy to defeat Satan's lies is to replace the lies with truth. Because the enemy exists, Christians are called to defend and teach God's truth, called apologetics, with the hope that *"God will grant them repentance leading them to a knowledge of the truth, and that they will come to their senses and escape from the trap of the devil, who has taken them captive to do His will"* (2 Timothy 2:25-26).

Bibliography

1. www.dwillard.org/articles
2. Dallas Willard, *The Divine Conspiracy: Rediscovering our Hidden Life in God* (New York: Harper Collin Publishers, 1998), 7.
3. The teachings of Marxism and totalitarianism deny the worth and freedom of the individual. Josh McDowell and Don Stewart, *Handbook of Today's Religions* (Nashville: Thomas Nelson Publishers, 1983), 449.
4. Chip Ingram, *The Invisible War* (Grand Rapids: Baker Publishing, 2006), 19-20.
5. Tony Evans, *The Truth about Angels and Demons* (Chicago: Moody Publishing, 2005), 10.
6. C. Fred Dickason, *Angels Elect and Evil* (Chicago: Moody Publishing, 1995), 164.
7. Evans, *The Truth about Angels and Demons*, 10-11.
8. Jerry Rankin, *Spiritual Warfare: The Battle for God's Glory* (Nashville Tennessee, B&H Publishing, 2009), 8.
9. Chip Ingram, *The Invisible War*, 46.
10. Peter J. Kreeft, *Handbook of Catholic Apologetics* (San Francisco: Ignatius Press, 2009), 23-24.
11. Peter Kreeft, *Handbook of Catholic Apologetics*, 24.
12. Philip E. Johnson: *The Right Questions: Truth, Meaning and Public Debate* (Downers Grove, IL: Intervarsity Press, 2002), 65.
13. Jerry Rankin, *Spiritual Warfare: The Battle for God's Glory*, 8.
14. Kenneth Wuest, *Wuest's Word Studies From the Greek New Testament* (Grand Rapids: Eerdmans Publishing, 1973), 94.
15. Sean McDowell et al., *Apologetics for a New Generation* (Eugene, Oregon: Harvest House Publishers, 2009), 17.
16. William Lane Craig et al., *To Everyone An Answer* (Downers Grove, IL: Intervarsity Press, 2004), 19.
17. Quoted in: *To Everyone An Answer*, 9.

18. Ken Samples, *Without a Doubt* (Grand Rapids, MI: Baker Books, 2004), 255-256.
19. Peter Kreeft, *Handbook of Catholic Apologetics*, 24.
20. Ibid., 24.
21. Ibid., 24.
22. Ted Honderrich ed., *The Oxford Companion to Philosophy* (New York: Oxford University Press, 2005), 49.
23. http://www.clayjones.net/2010/09/arguing-doesn%e2%80%99t-do-any-good-sure-it-does/
24. John MacArthur, *The MacArthur New Testament Commentary* (Chicago: Moody Press, 2003), 123-127.
25. Tony Evans, *Victory in Spiritual Warfare* (Eugene, Oregon: Harvest House Publishers, 2011), 55.
26. Suzanne Haneef, *What Everyone Should Know About Islam and Muslims* (Library of Islam, 1996), 20.
27. Caesar E. Farah, *Islam* (Hauppauge, New York: Barron's Educational Series, 1994), 95.
28. Josh McDowell, *Handbook of Today's Religions*, 395.
29. Quoted in Lee Strobel, *Finding the Real Jesus* (Grand Rapids: Zondervan, 2008), 71.
30. Ken Samples, *Without a Doubt*, 142-143.
31. Frank Turek, *I Don't Have Enough Faith To Be An Atheist* (Wheaton, Illinois: Crossway Books, 2004), 40-47.

About the Author

 Aaron Wentz is the Founder and President of the Michigan School of Apologetics (MSOA). MSOA exists to prepare people for eternity through confidence in the Christian worldview. And, equips people with life-changing tools to share the good news! MSOA holds six-week and weekend seminars all across Michigan in local churches, small groups, and campus ministries. At these seminars Christians learn:

- How apologetics can change your life
- Current cultural trends affecting the Church today
- How apologetics defeats spiritual warfare
- What is the gospel?
- How to share the gospel effectively with family and friends.
- How to share your faith without sounding offensive.
- How to respond when someone says "There is no absolute truth."
- How can Jesus be the only way?
- How to defend the Bible to a skeptic
- How to talk to an atheist
- Why does God allow evil?
- Is evolution true?
- What about those who have never heard about Jesus?
- What is the best evidence that Christianity is true?

At the end of the seminar, students will gain new confidence in their Christian faith, and how to share with family and friends. One student said, "I use to say nothing when my friends started talking about spiritual things, now I say 'bring it on!'"

Other Books by Author

Share with Confidence

A Simple Introduction to Christian Apologetics

Aaron Wentz

Some things in life are worth defending. People fight for their country and protect the things they believe are valuable. The Gospel of Jesus Christ is one of the most valuable realities worth defending. This noble effort of defending and protecting the Christian worldview is called apologetics. Through his book *Confidence to Share: A Simple Introduction to Christian Apologetics* Aaron Wentz shares easy methods to talk about God, defend the Bible, and get into spiritual conversations.

Other books will be coming in the near future.

Made in the USA
Columbia, SC
03 November 2021